Bibliographic information published by the German National Library:

The German National Library lists this publication in the National Bibliography; detailed bibliographic data are available on the Internet at http://dnb.dnb.de .

Imprint:

Copyright © 2016 GRIN Verlag, Open Publishing GmbH
Print and binding: Books on Demand GmbH, Norderstedt Germany
ISBN: 978-3-668-19359-8

This book at GRIN:

http://www.grin.com/en/e-book/319227/sherlock-holmes-in-the-novels-by-arthur-conan-doyle-and-his-modern-adaption

Pia Klaus

Sherlock Holmes in the novels by Arthur Conan Doyle and his modern adaption in the BBC TV-series "Sherlock"

GRIN Publishing

GRIN - Your knowledge has value

Since its foundation in 1998, GRIN has specialized in publishing academic texts by students, college teachers and other academics as e-book and printed book. The website www.grin.com is an ideal platform for presenting term papers, final papers, scientific essays, dissertations and specialist books.

Visit us on the internet:

http://www.grin.com/

http://www.facebook.com/grincom

http://www.twitter.com/grin_com

Table of Contents

1. Introduction

Plaid hat, pipe in the mouth and a magnifying glass in hand- this is today's image of the master-detective Sherlock Holmes. To be honest, Sir Arthur Conan Doyle's Holmes has never disappeared from our lives. And then there is the TV-channel BBC, which brought the hero into the televisions of twenty-first-century. Is this possible? Is the probably most famous crime character from the Victorian age survivable in London now? Work the legendary stories by Sir Arthur Conan Doyle today, too? Has Sherlock the instinct for the current high-tech-criminology? I like to answer these questions in the following elaboration.

First there will be a summary of Doyle's books and then a presentation of some TV-episodes will be given. At the end a comparison will bring the juxtaposition. Enjoy the track down for a historical hero in the modern civilisation!

2. Summary of the stories by Doyle

The figure of Sherlock Holmes was invented in 1887 by the doctor Sir Arthur Conan Doyle. Sherlock is the protagonist of all together 56 short-stories and four novels, written by Doyle. The first publication of all stories together was on 14th October 1892 in the book called "The Adventures of Sherlock Holmes". The individual stories had been serialised in "The Strand Magazine" between June 1891 and July 1892. They are not in a chronological order.[1]

The template for the detective Sherlock Holmes was the coroner and teacher of Doyle named Joseph Bell. The working-strategy of Holmes, the science of deduction, shows the euphoria for science in the 19th century.[2] This science includes the noticing of things that others simply do not observe. Holmes draws accurate conclusions about what he sees.[3] In Doyle's first Holmes story, "A study in Scarlet", the detective describes himself as someone who gets in the dumps as times an "[does not] open [his] mouth for days on end".[4]

---

[1] Cf. Deinert: The adventures.

[2] Cf. Bui: Sherlock vs. Holmes.

[3] Cf. Notari: summary & explanation.

[4] Doyle: Scarlet, page 11.

Sherlock Holmes works as a consulting detective, who helps the as very incompetent represented Scotland Yard. Holmes seems like a superman: he is fixed at reasons and shows nearly no interest in women. He is a big, gaunt guy wearing a Deerstalker hat and an inverness-coat. At home, in the 221B Baker-Street, he often wears his bathrobe.

Sherlock's staffer is Doctor Watson. They live together in the 221B Baker-Street, which in those days was fictional, until Watson marries and moves out. Doctor Watson is a former military doctor, who has served in Afghanistan. This soldier career forms a parallel to Doyle: He fought in the Second Anglo Boer War from 1896 to 1900.[5] Watson is important to the stories because he mainly compensates the brilliant and sometimes eccentric personality of Holmes. Most important is Watsons function as the narrator. He provides detailed written accounts of Sherlock's adventures for the readers to enjoy. Watson plays in the book the role of the reader through his many questions, he brings Holmes to explain his thoughts. This is a very smart technique of Doyle: Sherlock must always explain his discoveries to Watson, in turn, actually explaining them to the reader.[6]

3. The BBC-series

Different episodes with their connection to the literal original

A study in pink

The episode is about a murderous cab driver called Jeff in the TV-series and Jefferson Hope in the book. The parallel short-story is titled "A Study in Scarlet" and it was the first Sherlock-Holmes-story ever. The two plots are nearly the same. The cab driver murders several people. At first view these were looking like suicides, but when the third case happened in both versions the detective and the police are sure that the cases are linked. All people are killed by the cab driver by administering a lethal pill. In the end comes out that the victims always had a choice: The cab driver offers two pills, one poisoned one not. The selected passenger of Jeff, the prospective fatality, has to choose one of the pills and swallow her. For Jeff this method was always a possible suicide because he consumes the other pill. His felonies were caused by his sickness: he has an aneurysm, which can kill him every second. In the end he catches Sherlock. In his pres-

---

[5] Cf. Bui: Sherlock vs. Holmes.

[6] Cf. Notari: summary & explanation.

ence he dies, he was shot by Dr. Watson. The disease is the same in the book and in the series but in the book Dr. Watson find it out ("'Why', I cried, 'you have an aortic aneurism"[7]) and in the TV-version the cab driver explains his sickness ("Sherlock: 'You don't have long. Am I right?' Taxi Driver: 'Aneurism – right in here. Any breathe could be my last.' "[8])

The battle wounds of Doctor Watson also appear in both stories. But Doyle often slipped up when he wrote his stories. On closer inspection several contradictions stand out. In this first episode the wounds of Watson show this. In "A study in Scarlet", it is in his shoulder, in "A Sign of Four" it is in his leg an in "The Noble Bachelor" Watson limps. Steven Moffat's solution to this is the woundedness in both locations but the limp turns out to be psychosomatic.

A last similarity between the story in the book and in the series is the word "RACHE", which a victim wrote shortly before she dies. In the original novel, Doyle has Lestrade, the policemen, jump to the obvious conclusion that the victim was trying to write 'Rachel' but was unable to finish. Sherlock is of the opinion that the word is completed:" Rache is the german word for revenge".[9] In the episode this is reversed with the German-literate Anderson suggesting 'Rache' while Sherlock beliefs in 'Rachel'.[10]

The Blind Banker

The second case of Sherlock is about a mysterious code. In a great bank was a weird burglary. Nothing has been stolen but a painting has been destroyed through a mysterious sign. This sign is part of a code. It was addressed to the Hong-Kong-expert of the bank. This guy and a journalist are found death shortly afterwards. They both were killed under enigmatic circumstances and were members of the drug-smuggling Chinese organization Black Lotus. Holmes and Watson find this out with the help of the Chinese museum-employee. One of the two victims has stolen a part of the prey. The detective is firmly convinced that code is a book code. So he needs all the books from the flats of the victims for reading the code too. He cannot find the solution but he suspects the gang in the "Yellow Dragon Circus". Sherlock, Doctor Watson and his date Sarah Sawyer visit the circus. During the performance, Sherlock creeps behind the scenes to

---

[7] Doyle: Scarlet, page 148.

[8] A study in Pink.

[9] Doyle: Scarlet, page 145.

[10] A study in Pink.

4

search for clues. There he gets attacked by some gang members, but with the help of Watson and Sarah he escapes. While Sherlock does further researches, John and Sarah are getting kidnapped. Randomly Sherlock finds the matching book and can now decipher the code. He combines that the abductees have to stay in an old underground shaft. There the leader of the gang, General Shan, tries to extort Doctor Watson the location of the jade-needle because she mistook him with Sherlock. The detective can deliver them just in time but Shan escapes. The episode ends when Sherlock identifies the treasure as a thousand year old hairpin of a Chinese empress. The escaped Shan apologizes by a video message to a person called M. Shan then gets killed by a shot through a sniper. [11]

The parallel stories by Arthur Conan Doyle are "The Adventures of the Dancing Men" and "The Valley of Fear". In "The Adventures of the Dancing Men" the topic of the code appears. Thematised is the Sherlock's inability to decipher the code. He cannot do anything. [12] In the series he says that he "can't unravel it" [13]

The Great Game

With "The Great Game" Sherlock's private life becomes mixed up with his job. At first he lives in absolutely boredom. To be employed he shoots at a smiley face on the wall in his living-room. This scene forms a parallel to the literal original "The Adventure of the Musgrave Ritual". There Sherlock shoots at the phrase "V.R." which means Victoria reigns. [14] A second parallel is the blog of John Watson, in which the Doctor describes the life of the detective and also his bad site. Later he says that he would be lost without his blogger. [15] In Doyle's short-story "A Scandal in Bohemia" Sherlock says that he would be lost without his Boswell, the famous biographer of Samuel Johnson. [16] In the series then a mysterious riddle wakes him up: He is called to Scotland Yard where a mobile-phone looking very similar to one of "A Study in Scarlet", was delivered for him. With the phone he finds out that his task now is to solve five different crimes for saving five hostages. There Mark Gatiss, director of the TV-series used the motive of

---

[11] Cf. Erste: Banker.

[12] Cf. Doyle: Dancing men, page 21.

[13] The Blind Banker.

[14] Cf. Doyle: Dancing men, page 1.

[15] Cf. The Great Game.

[16] Cf. Doyle: Bohemia, page 10.

five pips like Coyle did it in "The Five Orange Pips"[17]. The signal of five pips is a warning one. It makes clear that something will happen again. The task was provided by Moriarty. After solving the last crime, Sherlock arranges a meeting in an indoor swimming-pool with him. Arrived at the pool, he meets unexpectedly on John. He wears also, like the other five victims, a bomb vest and repeats the words given to him. The both men are threatened by snipers. Then Moriarty appears. He explains that his purpose on the "game" was to show his power. He declares that another interference brings the deaths of not only Sherlock with it. Moriarty and the snipers first leave but then they come back. He announces that he would not let the two go yet. Sherlock responses with aiming at the bomb vest, from which he freed John shortly before. With this cliff-hanger the episode ends.[18]

A Scandal in Belgravia

In this sequence a woman comes in Sherlock's life the first time. The literal template is called "A Scandal in Bohemia". The TV-series begins with the resolution of the cliff-hanger of the last episode. Moriarty gets a call in which he receives a better offer and so he gives Sherlock and Doctor Watson their life and liberty. The next case of the detective-duet leads them to the high rows of Great Britain: They need to find the dominatrix Irene Adler, also known as "the woman" because she has some photos which show a member of the royal-house in action with Adler. The task now is to find these photos. In a first try Sherlock purloins the camera-phone, which is for Adler a medium of blackmail and also for her own security. They altogether overwhelm some CIA-agents and in a moment of inattention Adler injects Holmes a sedative and steals her phone back again. View months later Adler seemingly is killed. But this was only a trick for shaking off some enemies. Again CIA-agents threaten Sherlock and his personal sphere for receiving the camera-phone but Sherlock is able to overpower them again.

Later Adler needs Sherlock's help with a code. He deciphers it and helps in this way Adler's contact Moriarty: terrorists should be misled by control an airplane, which they wanted to blow up, remotely and only corpses as passengers. Mycroft, brother of Sherlock, client and owner of a high position in the British Government, confirms this. But by helping Moriarty indirectly, Sherlock has thwarted the deception. Adler exploits this situation and promotes her protection in exchange for some information from her phone.

---

[17] Cf. Doyle: Orange Pips, page 97.

[18] Cf. Nasrallah: Game.

Furthermore she scoffs about Sherlock and negates any feelings for him. Sherlock proves the contrary by unlocking her code[19]: "I am SHER-locked"[20] View months later Mycroft informs Watson about Adler's death in Pakistan through terrorists but in reality Sherlock saves her.[21]

"A Scandal in Bohemia" was published in 1895, the best year of Sherlock filled with his best cases. Vincent Starret, journalist, writes a poem about Sherlock and John: "though the world may explode, these two survive and it is always eighteen ninety-five"[22] In the TV-episode this number appears in the broken blog-counter of Watson's blog.[23]

The second parallel is the Deerstalker hat of Sherlock (see M1 in the appendix).

The most important parallel is Irene Adler. The dominatrix is made of the adventuress in the book. Sherlock cannot deduce anything from her appearance. She is an inscrutable and equal antagonist. She likes power-games, uses for blackmailing the collected information and she manipulates the detective. In the TV-episode she is defeated by Sherlock when he deciphers her mobile-phone-code. In Doyle's version they do not cultivate feelings of tender nature.[24] Moreover Sherlock has from the beginning respect for Adler. He recommends in both versions paying her. Also the victim of the woman is the same: A member of the royal house. In "A Scandal in Bohemia" it is her majesty herself[25] and in "A Scandal in Belgravia" it is a person of high significance.[26]

The Hounds of Baskerville

This time Henry Knight needs the help of Sherlock. The guy losts his father when he was a little boy. The father dies in the Dartmoor and was killed by a gigantic hound. Sherlock, who is interested by Henry's use of "hound" instead of "dog", and John accept the case. Henry tells John and Sherlock about the words "Liberty" and "In" in his dreams. For soling this case Sherlock and John go to Dartmoor, which is located near Baskerville, a Ministry of Defence research base. At the end Sherlock deduces a chemi-

---

[19] Cf. Téwon: Belgravia.

[20] A Scandal in Belgravia.

[21] Cf. Téwon: Belgravia.

[22] Allpoetry: 221b.

[23] Cf. A Scandal in Belgravia.

[24] Cf. Bui: Sherlock vs. Holmes.

[25] Cf. Doyle: Bohemia, page 15.

[26] Cf. A scandal in Belgravia.

cal weapon designed to trigger violent hallucinations was responsible for the gigantic dog. Retreating into his "mind palace", a memory technique, Sherlock realises "Liberty" and "In" stands for Liberty, Indiana. After viewing confidential files, he sees "Hound" was a secret CIA-project aimed at creating a hallucinatory anti-personnel weapon, but the project was abandoned several years before. Sherlock realises Frankland, an old friend of Henry's father who works at Baskerville and participated in the project, has continued it in secret. Frankland killed the father because he found him testing the drug. He wears a gas mask and a sweater with " Hound Liberty, In" during this act. A child is not able cope with this, so his mind tricked him. Every time Henry came back, Frankland gassed him with the hallucinogen. Frankland flees into a minefield and gets blown up. In the closing scene, Mycroft oversees the release of Jim Moriarty from a holding cell in which he has written Sherlock's name all over the walls.[27]

Like "A Scandal in Belgravia", "The Hounds of Baskerville" is very similar to its literal original. For example the sentence "Mr Holmes, they were footprints of gigantic hound!"[28] is exactly adopted. This sentence in both versions makes Sherlock interested.

The Reichenbach Fall

The season finale of season two is constructed by a flashback. John Watson reflects what three months earlier happened: Sherlock at this moment is a famous man. By solving numerous cases he gets much media attention. Especially for bringing back the Turner-painting "The Reichenbach Falls". The seemingly harmony is destroyed then by a criminal act of Moriarty. He opens the vault at the Bank of England and unlocks all the cells at Pentonville Prison. His purpose and message in this connection is getting Sherlock. For the underworld this message means that Sherlock has a special code, with which it is possible to bypass all security systems. Moriarty blackmails different people who are in connection to Sherlock's cases. They all work against the detective and so he is an enemy for Scotland Yard for the media and for the society. But Sherlock and John continue their work. Sherlock contacts Molly, his lover who works at the hospital. He makes her a declaration of love and asks her for help. Meanwhile John finds out that Mycroft divulged personal information about Sherlock at Moriarty. John finds Sherlock then at the Bart's lab but leaves after hearing Mrs Hudson, the subtenant of Sherlock and John, has been shot. Sherlock texts Moriarty that they meet on the roof of a hospital to

---

[27] Cf. Mevan: Baskerville.

[28] Doyle: Baskervilles, page 13.

resolve their "final problem". Moriarty reveals that there is no code, he just bribed security men, and that Sherlock must commit suicide or Moriarty's assassins will kill John, Mrs Hudson and Lestrade. Sherlock realises that Moriarty has a fail-safe and can call the killings off. Then he convinces Moriarty that he is willing to do anything to make him activate the fail-safe, after acknowledging that he and Sherlock are alike, Moriarty tells Sherlock that only the condition of him staying alive can save the life of the hostages. Then he commits suicide by shooting himself in the mouth. With no way to use the fail-safe, Sherlock calls John, who is rushing back from 221B Baker Street after realising the report about Mrs Hudson's death was a ruse. Claiming that he was always a fake and explaining this last phone call is his "note", Sherlock throws himself from the roof of St Bartholomew's Hospital as John looks on from the street, thereby ensuring that Moriarty's true identity dies with him. After being knocked to the ground by a cyclist, John stumbles over to watch, in a daze, as Sherlock's bloody body is carried away by hospital staff. The episode returns to John's therapy session, where he is unable to open up. Mycroft is shown reading the tabloid newspaper "The Sun" with a front page headline "Suicide of Fake Genius." Later, John visits Sherlock's grave with Mrs Hudson. There, he reaffirms his faith in Sherlock and begs him not to be dead. As he walks away, Sherlock looks on from the shadows before also walking away.[29]

The literal version is called "The Final Problem". Therein Sherlock Doyle wanted to be done with his character: He lets him die. In the TV-episode this seems so first too but in the end the viewer sees Sherlock alive. So he is just for the people in the series a death man. What also in both versions appears is the fact that Sherlock seems to become more and more aware of the danger he is in and the danger he might bring to his personal surroundings.[30] In the end he declares his total life and his job as a fake show. He created his cases and his enemies for having fun and an employment.[31]

This episode assumes in both variations knowledge of Sherlock's character. It presents himself and his near reference to his friends. Especially to Watson, a lonely man who went a long way from the bottom, broken place, in which Sherlock first found him.[32]

---

[29] Cf. Pragueimp: Reichenbach.

[30] Cf. Stokes: Reichenbach.

[31] Cf. Doyle: Final, page 6; Cf. The Reichenbach Fall.

[32] Cf. Stokes: Reichenbach.

The producers Steven Moffat, Mark Gatiss and Sue Vertue looked for a tall and thin guy as Sherlock. They watched the film "Atonement", in which Benedict Cumberbatch had a role, and knew that he is the perfect person for Sherlock. The look of Cumberbatch was as suitable as it not better can be. For his preparation for the role he informs himself by the literal original. His task in the series was it to show Sherlock's cleverness. He is able to do what no computer can do: He looks at a crime scene, uses his mind as a computer and links a narrative intuitively on first receiving all of that information. Benedict Cumberbatch has to connect mental cleverness with the presence of a modern multimedia-hero. Embodying this he was very successful because of his physical presence and his way of reasoning and analysing which is second to none.

Casting the partner of Sherlock, Doctor John Watson, was more difficult. The producers searched for a person that could create the physical and emotional contrast between Sherlock and John well. Martin Freeman as Watson and Benedict Cumberbatch as Holmes immediately looked like the famous detective duo. Freeman's specialty in playing ordinary people was the decisive reason for choosing him as the ordinary Doctor John Watson. He brings him absolutely truthful and honest to the viewer, not making him more colourful for more interest.

Based on the differences in their characters, Cumberbatch and Freeman are the perfect couple for their roles. The mixture of their behaviours makes the series to what it is now.[33]

4. Comparison of the book and the TV-series

In general Mark Gatiss and Steven Moffat created a slightly different and also equal story to the literal adventures of Sherlock Holmes by Sir Arthur Conan Doyle. They kept the main characteristics: a duet composed of a detective and a doctor are solving mysterious crimes. The actions take place in London and the two protagonists share a flat together. Although the plot takes place in the same city, the era is different. The current Sherlock is more contemporary. When the "old" Sherlock relies on his brain, the "young" one combines this with new technologies. The literal detective always welcomes his clients warmly, listens at them patiently and is more looking for the welfare

---

[33] Cf. Tribe: Chronicles, page 40 to 51.

of them. The revised one is a rough man, completely selfish, quite show-off, he only chooses his surveys depending on his own desire and the complexity of it. For him it is not possible accepting he is wrong and he is totally aware of his genius and does not mind to prove this. Watson's role in both plots is to support Sherlock but also offering the audience an opportunity to understand Sherlock. He brings Sherlock's humanity to the people. Both Watson's were wounded during a war but when the first one suffered from enteric fever, the second one is shell shocked after his injury and keeps a psychological pain in his leg. The relationship between those two protagonists is in both versions a common factor. A strong friendship links the two men: Watson always beliefs in Sherlock who just slowly changes his selfish behaviour. Another important character is the enemy of Sherlock: Moriarty. He is younger than in the book and the writers of the series also changed his character: They described him as a rather dull, rather posh villain person who acts like an absolute psycho. For Doyle he is the "Napoleon of crime", an old evil genius. Moriarty's power makes him be able to do anything without being afraid of some consequences. This ability makes Sherlock interested in him. He sees himself, looking at him. In the book and also in the TV-version Moriarty is the way to kill Sherlock.[34] The new Sherlock series is a modernized and true to the source mirror one. It is an update of the elements by holding true to the essence of the stories and the characters. Apart from smaller signs to the original, for example the title, and little allusions to characteristic conversations, there are many larger plot-elements from the original, which can be found in the series story. Often these things are set into a rather different context or are parodied. The episodes are definitively inspired by the original stories to a large percentage but they still differentiate from Doyle's ideas, not only by modernization but also through combining elements in interesting and very unique ways.[35] Doyle wrote during his lifetime a revolutionary story, which created recognition and fame to the audience. The people were impressed, at that time like today. Gatiss and Moffat used the charm of revising an old book. They brought the flair of the 1880's, the absolute impression and acknowledgment, back.[36]

---

[34] Cf. Bui: Sherlock vs. Holmes.

[35] Cf. Liath: Relate.

[36] Cf. Bhoraskar: Comparing.

5. Conclusion

The most important thing to say is that Sherlock settles in our society trouble-free in. Mark Gatiss and Steven Moffat kept the essential from the original story written by Sir Arthur Conan Doyle. In their TV-series even though is in many ways different but Sherlock's appearance still is characterized by his rudeness and his callousness. The producers of the series brought Sherlock Holmes back and with him the enthusiasm for crazy guys and mysterious crime-riddles. They created a new Sherlock Holmes with the improved and modernized characteristics. The ardour for the series is also caused by the great performance of Benedict Cumberbatch, Martin Freeman and their colleagues. Together they produced another historical detective series. This success is also based on the timeless writing style of Doyle. He was the initiator of Sherlock. He is his inventor. He gave all the producers of some Sherlock series their main idea. Without him, there would not be such a pleasure for Holmes and his adventures. In my opinion the two protagonists personify the true meaning of friendship. They show people, during Doyle's times and also today, what friendship can effect. This is a point that the whole audience should take with them. Together we can achieve all goals and we can solve all problems. This is what I take with me. And also that the idea of one man in the 19th century can affect people in different time periods, is a point which I will not forget. "Eliminate all other factors, and the one which remains must be the truth!" With this in mind we see that in all of us a little Sherlock works.

6. Bibliography

A Scandal in Belgravia. Script Moffat Steven. Direction McGuigan Paul. Actors Cumberbatch Benedict, Freeman Martin. Producer Vertue Sue. Sherlock. Season 2, episode 1. BBC. London, Great Britain, 2012. TV-series-episode [cited as A Scandal in Belgravia].

A Study in Pink. Script Moffat Steven. Direction McGuigan Paul. Actors Cumberbatch Benedict, Freeman Martin. Producer Vertue Sue. Sherlock. Season 1, episode 1. BBC. London, Great Britain, 2010. TV-series-episode [cited as A study in Pink].

ADAMS, GUY: Sherlock- The Casebook, London, 2012.

Allpoetry: 221b, http://allpoetry.com/poem/8599039-221b-by-Vincent-Starrett, state: 06.01.16 [cited as Allpoetry: 221b].

Amber Stokes, The Final Problem/The Reichenbach Fall - The End of Sherlock Season 2, http://seasonsofhumility.blogspot.de/2012/05/final-problemthe-reichenbach-fall-end.html, state: 07.01.16 [cited as Stokes: Reichenbach].

Chloé, Comparison: Original Sherlock vs BBC Sherlock, http://ticketybooo.blogspot.de/2013/05/comparison-original-sherlock-vs-bbc.html, state: 07.01.16.

CONAN DOYLE, SIR ARTHUR: A Study in Scarlet and the Sign of the Four, London, 2005 [cited as Doyle: Scarlet].

CONAN DOYLE, SIR ARTHUR: The hounds of Baskervilles, New York, 1994 [cited as Doyle: Baskervilles].

CONAN DOYLE, SIR ARTHUR: A scandal in Bohemia, Spain, 2015 [cited as Doyle: Bohemia].

CONAN DOYLE, SIR ARTHUR: The adventure of the dancing men and other Sherlock Holmes stories, New York, 1997 [cited as Doyle: Dancing men].

CONAN DOYLE, SIR ARTHUR: The adventures and memoirs of Sherlock Holmes, Toronto, 2002 [cited as Doyle: Orange Pips].

CONAN DOYLE, SIR ARTHUR: The Final Problem, London, 2012 [cited as Doyle: Final].

Debbie Notari, Adventures of Sherlock Holmes by Arthur Conan Doyle: Summary & Explanation, http://study.com/academy/lesson/adventures-of-sherlock-holmes-by-arthur-conan-doyle-summary-lesson-quiz.html, state: 07.01.16 [cited as Notari: summary & explanation].

Horst Deinert, The Adventures of Sherlock Holmes, https://en.wikipedia.org/wiki/The_Adventures_of_Sherlock_Holmes, state: 07.01.16 [cited as Deinert: The adventures].

Liath, How closely do Sherlock Episodes relate to the original stories?, http://movies.stackexchange.com/questions/12587/how-closely-do-sherlock-episodes-relate-to-the-original-stories?answertab=active#tab-top, state: 07.01.16 [cited as Liath: Relate].

Lily Mevan, The Hounds of Baskerville, https://en.wikipedia.org/wiki/The_Hounds_of_Baskerville, state 06.01.16 [cited as Mevan: Baskerville].

M.Bui, Sherlock vs. Holmes: Ein Vergleich der BBC-Serie mit den Geschichten von A.C.Doyle, https://storify.com/MBui_Sbg/sherlock-vs-holmesein-vergleich-der-bbc-serie-mit, state: 07.01.16 [cited as Bui: Sherlock vs. Holmes].

MaryAnn Johanson: Sherlock's deerstalker, http://www.flickfilosopher.com/wptest/wp-content/uploads/2012/01/sherlockdeerstalker2.gif, state: 06.01.16.

Mohammad Nasrallah: The Great Game (Sherlock), https://en.wikipedia.org/wiki/The_Great_Game_(Sherlock), state 05.01.16 [cited as Nasrallah: Game].

Pragueimp, The Reichenbach Fall, https://en.wikipedia.org/wiki/The_Reichenbach_Fall, state: 06.01.16 [cited as Pragueimp: Reichenbach].

Print Collector, The Adventure of Silver Blaze, Holmes questioning a suspect. Encounter between Silas Brown, the trainer who was hiding the lost racehorse Silver Blaze, and Holmes. Arthur Conan Doyle's story published in The Strand Magazine, London, 1892, illustrated by Sidney E. Paget, http://www.gettyimages.ca/detail/news-photo/the-adventure-of-silver-blaze-holmes-questioning-a-suspect-news-photo/463896807, state: 06.01.16.

Ravi Bhoraskar, Faithful to the Original: Comparing Sherlock and Sherlock Holmes, https://blogbloggityblog.wordpress.com/2012/03/03/faithful-to-the-original-comparing-sherlock-and-sherlock-holmes/, state: 07.01.16 [cited as Bhoraskar: Comparing].

Sohn Téwon: A Scandal in Belgravia, https://en.wikipedia.org/wiki/A_Scandal_in_Belgravia, state 06.01.16 [cited as Téwon: Belgravia].

The Blind Banker. Script Thompson Steve. Direction Lyn Euros. Actors Cumberbatch Benedict, Freeman Martin. Producer Vertue Sue. Sherlock. Season 1, episode 2. BBC. London, Great Britain, 2010. TV-series-episode [cited as The Blind Banker].

The Great Game. Script Gatiss Mark. Direction McGuigan Paul. Actors Cumberbatch Benedict, Freeman Martin. Producer Vertue Sue. Sherlock. Season 1, episode 3. BBC. London, Great Britain, 2010. TV-series-episode [cited as The Great Game].

The Hounds of Baskerville. Script Gatiss Mark. Direction McGuigan Paul. Actors Cumberbatch Benedict, Freeman Martin. Producer Vertue Sue. Sherlock. Season 2, episode 2. BBC. London, Great Britain, 2012. TV-series-episode.

The Reichenbach Fall. Script Thompson Steve. Direction Haynes Toby. Actors Cumberbatch Benedict, Freeman Martin. Producer Cameron Elaine. Sherlock. Season 2, episode 3. BBC. London, Great Britain, 2012. TV-series-episode [cited as The Reichenbach Fall].

TRIBE, STEVE: Sherlock- Chronicles, London, 2014 [cited as Tribe: Chronicles.

Zuschauerredaktion Das Erste: Der blinde Banker, http://www.daserste.de/unterhaltung/film/sherlock/sendung/der-blinde-banker-110.html , state 05.01. 2016 [cited as Erste: Banker]